MOSSES AND LICHENS

MOSSES AND LICHENS

DEVIN JOHNSTON

FARRAR, STRAUS AND GIROUX
NEW YORK

Farrar, Straus and Giroux

175 Varick Street, New York 10014

Copyright © 2019 by Devin Johnston

All rights reserved

Printed in the United States of America

First edition, 2019

Library of Congress Cataloging-in-Publication Data

Names: Johnston, Devin, author.

Title: Mosses and lichens : poems / Devin Johnston.

Description: First edition. | New York : Farrar, Straus and Giroux, 2019.

Identifiers: LCCN 2018048701 | ISBN 9780374213497 (hardcover)

Subjects: LCSH: American poetry—21st century.

Classification: LCC PS3610.O385 A6 2019 | DDC 811/.6—dc23

LC record available at https://lccn.loc.gov/2018048701

Designed by Quemadura

Our books may be purchased in bulk for promotional, educational,
or business use. Please contact your local bookseller or the Macmillan
Corporate and Premium Sales Department at 1-800-221-7945, extension
5442, or by e-mail at MacmillanSpecialMarkets@macmillan.com.

www.fsgbooks.com
www.twitter.com/fsgbooks
www.facebook.com/fsgbooks

1 3 5 7 9 10 8 6 4 2

CONTENTS

MOSSES AND LICHENS

SLOW SPRING

Not days of anger
but days of irritation,
light through dirty glass,
songs of horse and rider,
tornado sirens
for a storm that rumbles past
but finds no clear rotation.

Not days of anger
but days of slow connection,
days of snow geese passing
north above the river,
days of eros
endlessly drawn out
through error and confusion.

Not days of anger
but days of indirection,
contrails like
cathedral arches
and rumor of morels,
days without a strike,
days of binding arbitration.

Not days of anger
but days of mild congestion,
infants of inconstant sorrow,
days of foam in gutters,
blossoms and snow
mingling where they fall,
a spring of cold profusion.

Grant but as many sorts of mind as moss
spread in profuse and tender shade
across the face of a granite block
that came to rest in the last ice age;
a buoyant clump of cushion moss,
the nap of sheet moss, fit for sleep,
a bog of sphagnum, shirred and soft,
along the bed of Pickle Creek.
Carpet mosses, loose yet dense,
absorb a day of steady rain,
pervasive, yet so reticent
that many have no common names.

More subtle still, an areole
of lichen lives on rock and air,
the crust of paint on a coping stone,
an orange blaze that marks no trail;
a flake of ancient bronze, an ash
that powders the fingertips like sage;
the reindeer lichen's tangled mass
of antler branches, brow and bay.
Across the valley floor, the like
adapt to every circumstance

as through a mesh of dappled light,
a lichen clings to every surface.

A row of oaks may call to mind
an ancient marble colonnade
at Samothrace, a mountainside
where shadows cleanly separate
in flutes around a fallen drum
and gods in golden ratios
still subdivide the setting sun
through one remaining portico.

But here the lines of sight get lost
in undergrowth, a sandstone shelf
fogged with lichen, furred with moss
so thick along the water's edge
a falling walnut makes no thud.
Approaching fifty, Ruskin turned
his mind to moss, and taking up
a shaggy brick from the yard, observed
the leaves that die invisibly
and turn to humus, dark and wet,
remains that steadily accrete
beneath the bright ascending crest.

CLYDE'S DRAWING

A pair of lizards,
rough yet lithe,
cavorts in a field
to fiddle music,
scales enflamed
by the rising sun.
King kong kitchie
kitchie ki⁓me⁓o!

Whatever comes after
moves more slowly
to fill the ground
with a bit of color,
blue and green
scribbles of prostrate
knotweed, scratches
of dog fennel,
chopped strokes
of cheatgrass,
loops of plantain
and stars of thistle,
cold life never stirred
to saurian quickness.

At nightfall
under a hooded lamp
the hand takes
a thousand paths
from leaf to leaf:
chapped lines
of crayon sprawl
across the page,
smudges of daylight
lost in the weeds.

NEIGHBORS

These days I work from home,
grading folk and blues LPs
in a little room upstairs
facing the back, a gable end
stooped over its own wedge
of morning shadow.
Down in the yard a sheet billows;
a squirrel hunches over a dish
of sunflower seeds
while a hawk wheels overhead.
This arrangement looks precarious
and yet maintains a sort of stasis,
rhythms oddly stable,
brick alley, ragged hedge,
and fences of warped cedar board
bound by tangles of infrastructure,
blocks and lines
of telephone and cable.

At least four times a day
a blue Jeep Cherokee
with paper plates rattles past,

returning minutes later.
Each circuit forms a link
in a chain that runs
from the Golden Crescent
through the hawsepipe
of a cargo ship
and down through ocean depths
to a private darkness
never brought to light.
Taking out the trash,
I've seen those tinted windows
parked behind the duplex,
engine softly pinging.

Out front, a sleek sedan pulls up
and idles beside a fire hydrant
until a young Somali woman
steps from the stoop
and sidles to the driver's side,
adjusting her golden scarf.
She carries a clamshell take-out box
that she passes through the window,
pats the car, and it pulls off
(heroin, or sambusas
from some unlicensed enterprise?).

Nothing stirs along the block,
empty but for the two of us,
neighbors still at school or work.
Heavy lintels darken the doors,
the afternoon half gone.
The sun would never never never
the needle skips upstairs.
Turning, she catches my eye
and smiles. *Ma gaajoonaysaa?*
Uncertain what
she's asked or offered,
I simply nod and head inside.

ACTAEON

AFTER OVID

There was a mountain full of blinds,
the upland stained with trails of blood
by noon, when shadows of things contract
to slips and leave no cover.
Then Actaeon, pausing to rest
beneath an oak, addressed those men
who stalked the wilderness with him.
My friends, we've shot the limit:
Our bags are full of game,
our buck knives streaked with blood;
the day held luck enough. Another dawn
when shadows still lie cool and long
we'll try these grounds again. For now,
the sun has reached its height
and cracks the fields with heat.
Let's quit, and gather up the nets.
The men obeyed and turned for home,
the prince by a separate path alone.

There was a valley dense with spruce
and Tuscan cypress, sacred to
Diana, goddess of the hunt
and all things wild and reticent.
Hidden in her deepest wood
there lay a cave, much like the grottos
found in rococo retreats
Where Drops from Mineral Roofs distill,
And Crystals break the sparkling Rill—
a limestone arch, through which a stream
descended, bickering over stones,
and flowed into a water hole
encircled by a mantle of moss.
Here the goddess would bathe her limbs
after the hunt, and cool her skin
in the clear water, handing her bow
and arrows to her armor-bearer,
then slipping off her clothes and shoes
as she stepped down into the pool.
The one called Strand, a windswept nymph
and quickest of her retinue,
would gather up Diana's hair
and wind it in a sleek bun
to keep it dry, although her own

fell loose about her shoulders.
Cloud and Crystal, Drop and Shower
would fill their urns to drench the goddess
as she stood in their midst undressed.

Meanwhile, with no more thought of hunting,
Actaeon had lost his bearings
and wandered through Diana's wood
until he stumbled on her bower,
led by fate; and when he entered
through a mist of falling water,
the nymphs began to beat their breasts,
and the forest echoed with their shrieks.
All poured round to cover the goddess,
though she stood taller than the rest
by head and shoulders, like a peak
above the clouds; and like a cloud
struck by shafts of the setting sun
or rosy-fingered dawn, she blushed,
and though in the midst of turbulence,
she turned aside and dropped her gaze.
He! He! Her fingers itched
for an arrow to draw and loose.
She cupped her hand and flung a scoop
of water in the stranger's face,

dousing his hair as she spoke this curse
of catastrophes to come:
Now say you've seen my naked flesh!
Go on, tell anyone you can.

With no more words, she summoned forth
from the damp patches on his head
the beams and branching tines of antlers,
and stretched his neck and pricked his ears.
She turned his hands to cloven hooves
and upper arms to slender thighs,
enveloping his body
in a hide of dappled fur.
She sent a sudden surge of fear
through his veins: he leapt and fled,
wondering at his own speed
until he glimpsed his antlered head
reflected in a little stream.
He mouthed *My God*, but no voice came,
only a bellow where his voice had been,
and tears streamed down what were his cheeks;
his mind alone remained unchanged.
What should he do? Strike out for home,
the safety of those palace walls,
or bed down in the open air?

He hesitated, caught between
a path of shame and one of fear.

As he stood in doubt, he saw the hounds
come down the slope, first Blue and Frost,
coonhounds both and keen of scent,
creatures of one fixed pursuit.
Then like a storm the others came,
all-consuming, keen of sight,
the deer- and wolfhounds, purebred coursers,
tall and swift as deer, and lurchers
bred from hounds and rough-haired collies,
and wolfdogs running silently
amid a raucous froth of curs,
chop- and bawl-mouthed, at full cry.
Dread, Jolly, Wheeler, Strike:
each bore a name to suit its nature,
too many to pause and list them here.
Eagerly the pack gave chase
along a ridge and through a gorge
on trails so rough they disappeared
in scree, and still the dogs pursued.

He fled across the grounds he'd hunted,
in flight from those he once commanded,

and tried to shout over his shoulder,
I'm Actaeon! Obey your master!
No words came through his open mouth;
the sound of baying filled the air.
First Whirlwind, quickest of the pack,
leapt and fastened on his neck,
then Drum and Fury bit his haunch
and held on as the rest caught up
and clamped their teeth into his hide,
leaving no fur free of blood.
He brayed, a sound not quite human
and not quite what a stag would make,
but clearly signaling distress,
filling the gorge with his lament;
then staggered to his foreknees, bowed
as if in silent prayer for aid.

And yet his friends, oblivious,
urged on the pack with *Harrk-forrard!*
and glanced about for Actaeon,
and called with cupped hands, *Aaactaeon!*
as if he were not there. He heard,
and turned his head as they complained,
He must be lagging on the trail,
too bad he missed the spectacle.

Of course, he'd rather have missed out,
and he would rather have seen than felt
the dreadful things his dogs had done.
From everywhere they circled round,
their muzzles buried in his flesh,
and tore apart their master,
whatever trace of him endured
beneath the semblance of a deer.

CONTACT

Felt before seen:
not the numb blooming of an itch
but needle prick, the *spritzig* sting
of anesthetic in her spit,
an effervescent prickle.

If seen, a mere sketch,
a whisker of brush at dusk
against the standing night
of old growth from the Age of Pine.

Tiger striped, they swarmed the skin
of voyageurs and martyrs,
a misery from which
the Jesuits found no escape
but to run always without stopping.

Surrounded by smoke and dogs,
Father Chabanel
rarely left the longhouse,
yet through a thousand bites
spread his blood upon the waters,

the iron-tinted
lakes and kettle bogs
in which mosquitoes incubate.

In the shallows, Hurons
would wade at leisure
and soothe their wheals,
coating their legs with wet clay.

Fingers impatient
with the buttons of a shirt,
desperate to shed
accustomed constraints,
you strip down
as if aflame,
then pause demurely
to hang your clothes
on a crown
of upturned roots.

How is it? *Cold!*
wading through
foam and twigs,
caught between
desire and lassitude,
having kept
apart too long.
A current wrinkles

around your legs
and the river lifts
above itself
as fog.

The wind picks up, and a few raindrops
flick the river's surface.
Through trees unmodified by leaves
a makeshift town takes shape
from tents, RVs, and caravans
strung with Christmas lights and equipped
with all the comforts of home.
Section One has filled,
a stolid cul-de-sac
of bicycles and woodsmoke,
parakeets and radios,
a garden gnome beside one truck,
its cursive legend burnt in pine:
Welcome, stranger, to this place.

In darkness at the outer edge,
two teens have pitched their tent,
ill prepared, a little stoned,
discordant over poor provisions
and the wet scrape of a match.
—*Why'd you even come*
when all you do is bitch?

—I wanted us to be together.
They pass an apple back and forth
and toss away the core,
then cede their picnic table
to a family of raccoons,
crawling through tent flaps
to the gentle whirr of zippers
and whispers of remorse.
At the edge of quiet hours,
the girl begins to moan
Fuck me! Fuck me! over and over
across adjacent sites
for everyone to hear,
command or exclamation,
goad or shame, asking and getting
simultaneous but not the same.

APOCRYPHA

He woke an hour before the dawn
stiff and cold and clarified,
unsure how long he had been gone,
unsure of all save that he'd died.
All those nights of sleeping rough
and mornings building toward a migraine,
too many deserts, not enough
Pacific waters pricked with rain.
Lift a stone, you'll find me there:
but no one could, and no one did.
Whatever he'd exposed to air
now lay within a pyramid.
He woke before the crack of dawn
to watch the dark divide
and ebb across a strand of stone
as the light solidified:
a treetop splintered into crows;
a surfer rode a crest of foam.
From a bed of lithic sand, he rose
and took his slow way home
through narrow streets and past an inn
deserted, at the edge of town;

a voice from somewhere deep within
repeated and prolonged a sound.
It might have been *ammam* or *um*,
a bit of Greek or Arabic,
the sort of muffled sounds that hum
through several feet of brick.
Never a father, always the son,
he had no living family,
not far to go, no longer young,
but finally clean at thirty-three.

COVER SONGS

In March, along the avenue
still flecked with frost,
we don't mind
trudging through
the slow churn
of pigeons
and anklets of exhaust.

Overhead, a hawk
patrols the long trough
between rooftop and rooftop,
alert to what
lies exposed.
As dusk turns to dark,
the band picks up
where it left off,

up a battered staircase
and through adjacent gloom
to a padlocked
rehearsal space
soundproofed with foam.

Once inside, nobody stops:
long custom requires
rowing steadily
above the pops
and thermal hiss
of amplifiers.

No, we don't mind
with day gone
singing words that anyone
would be ashamed
to speak, no choice
but to sing them with conviction.

DOMESTIC SCENES

A spray of toothbrushes,
stems in a mug:
a family portrait.

■

In dirty light, disordered pairs
of snow boots and galoshes
line the welcome mat:

the stragglers have come home
and passed inward on stocking feet
to the apartment's hidden core.

■

With eyes shut, the child
twirls on the kitchen tile,
a whirling dervish
turning continuously
toward herself

like the spindle
on a phonograph
until she wobbles,
drunk with vertigo;
another song
about a baby
and a bottle
ends with a crash.

■

Alone in his room
the youngest one
dreams of whatever
takes place while
he sleeps—the flutter
of a distant storm,
the clink of cups,
a midnight visitor—
and wakes to tell
what we already know.

■

Nothing that we plant thrives here.
Dead wood advances down
our rose stems year by year.
And yet the honeyvine, a weed,
curls around the base
and climbs with mindless mastery
to reach a waving height
free of thorns and shade.
There, it hangs an anglepod
to feed on the morning light.

MARRIAGE

At the lowest stratum of Troy,
beneath the Scaean Gates
and broken dishes and bronze flakes
as brittle as fallen leaves,
Schliemann found a pair of toads
in hibernation since the time
of Hector and Andromache.
To think of what survives!

PACHELBEL'S CANON

A string quartet performs in the gym
at FCI Greenville Camp for women,
musicians in black on folding chairs,
the women on risers lounging at ease
in the current of air from a drum fan,
tapping their feet and whispering
behind their hands, amused to know
from diamond commercials and white sales
the same eight notes in eight measures
in rounds with basso continuo—
a blues for late afternoon,
tenderness and irony
so tightly wound and wedded that
they form a braid without break.
Summer slowly turns to autumn;
an air of waiting descends on the gym
as when a congregation waits
for the missing bride or groom.

AN EPOCH

Each streetlight declares an absence
where it pools, a square of sidewalk
poured long ago and still engraved
with the burr of a trowel
and rough swirls of a broom,
the curb edge sprayed
with neon glyphs of hook and arrow
that do not pertain to us.
Only the light's vapor has changed
from mercury to sodium,
a spectral shift from blue to orange.
Matte black, a lone beetle
churns across the concrete
beneath its upturned shield.

LIBERTY SALVAGE

It was a good house,
good enough
for any who called it home,
battered by storms
and baked by the sun,
gently creaking
through the dark
and rattling as the sun rose
for nights and days
past reckoning or recall.
Everything goes,
copper wire
stripped by thieves,
bricks knocked loose
one by one
and sold as salvage,
foundations
now a faint impression.

And yet the key,
so much a part of you
it turned
thoughtlessly,
still hangs on your ring.

A SMALL KINGDOM

Come on, let's start, there's work to be done,
constructing battlements from blocks
and a castle keep from cardboard.
I play my part, a supporting role
building road across the carpet,
its wool obscured by a cloud of dust,
elephants on the march,
their buttery plastic almost edible.
These are the Alps, and this the col,
a fold in the quilt from which a wolf
howls and hurls its paper rocks
down on dinosaurs and mammals,
a phalanx of anachronisms
borne of circumstance and whim.

I play my part with half a mind,
ironies and violence held at bay,
until the phone rings: an old friend
whose wife has finally tossed him out
needs help moving, boxes by the curb.
I've been there, and recommend
a furnished room a few blocks distant.

Come back, let's play! This is a harbor town,
and on its wharf, a whittled ship
outward bound with a load of apples.
I once lived here, but now I wait
for a chance to slip away.

Holy Mary, Mother of God!
Back and forth
across the wood
before an empty
stage, a squad
of Archangels
beats the trap

until the ball gets loose
and the architecture rings
with shrill cries
and squeaking shoes.

Hail Mary, full of grace!
Among so many
lines and boundaries
Natalia kneels
to tie a lace
over, under,
around, and through,

attending to her task
with painstaking care
as five Dragons
thunder past.

THROWN OBJECT

Give me that! Give me that!
Okay, go and get it.

■

She fell
He pushed

by accident
on purpose

■

One seethes, the other floats;
A whisper detonates a cry.

THE YOLK

Embryo clicks to embryo
and twitters like a pipistrelle.
One ear, curled against the breast,
amplifies a rapid tempo.
The other, cupped against the shell,
detects a rustle near the nest.

One eye, dark as anthracite,
will someday seek a hiding place.
The other, dimly sensing light,
will watch for predators on high.
The brain, the brain separates
into hemispheres of earth and sky.

The kids pause beside a bluff
to touch its bands of sediment—
soft silt of an inland sea
or vast lagoon, now thin and rough
as deckle edges of a book,
epochs compressed to signatures
cockled with faults and folds—
and wonder which pertain to us.
Were any people here back then?
Before the answer comes, they bolt
and race each other down the trail
through a ravine of moss and lichen
to splash across a shallow creek,
still of an age that has no end.

BEFORE A STORM

a spring night
talking
together

lighting
one cigarette
with another

■

given a porch light
and breath of wind
shadows run riot

■

a slug of rain
splash of water

panache

the crinkle of
wrapping paper

■

a high-performance engine
dipped in copper sulfate
and furred with blue crystals

■

in the wind and gloom
not a bounding line
but mass and tone
not violin
but pipe organ
not definition
but thick emotion

■

at rest: a knife
within its sheath

HIGH WATER

AFTER OVID

April shuts the north wind
and whatever blast puts clouds to flight
in limestone caves, a low whine,
and then sets loose the south wind
to flap on damp and heavy wings,
ghastly face obscured by fog,
beard sodden with pouring rain.
Froth flows from his white locks
and dew drips from shreds and feathers.
When his wide palms percuss a cloud,
the pressure makes a thunderclap
and wrings a torrent from a sop.
At his tail, an arc arrayed
in faint prismatic colors
forms a flying buttress.
Stalks lie flattened, and farmers cast
querulous voices across the fields,
another year come to nothing.

At last the sky begins to clear,
but the hoop of sky does not describe

the limit of the storm's force:
the Mississippi rises, and calls
three rivers to a confluence,
commanding tributaries to crest:
Turn all your strength to violence.
Roll and tumble! Loosen the reins
and drive your waters down the line.
Springs gush, backwaters rise;
they roll and tumble down the line
from mountain source to delta mouth.
Soon the Mississippi itself
breaches levees at three points,
bursting through with a splay of debris,
floods fanning across the plains.
Crops, orchards, cattle, sheds,
and people all get washed away,
along with churches and their gods.
If any house remains upright,
built on such a firm foundation,
water rises over its eaves
until its chimneys disappear,
hid beneath a broad abyss.
Now gulf and coast lose all distinction:
shores absent, all is ocean,
a ruffled surface without end.

Some folks take to hilltops,
others perch on thwarts of a skiff
and row where they once plowed.
One sails over fields of corn
and over the roof of a sunken barn;
another hooks a spotted bass
in the crown of a cottonwood.
His anchor catches the valley floor,
his keel scrapes a hidden trellis.
Where herds of horses cropped the grass
sturgeons rest their pale bellies.
Nosing through a brackish world,
sea creatures well might wonder
at the parks and suburbs underwater.
Dolphins occupy the woods:
they course through upper branches
and bump against the stirred oaks.
Wolf and lamb go down together,
predator and prey pell-mell.
Despite the boar's lightning speed
it churns foam helplessly,
and the deer's hooves find no traction.
Pigeons search on weary wings
for any earth on which to settle
until they fall into the ocean.

No longer bound by shores,
waves have overwhelmed the hills
and new waves like rolling thunder
break against the highest peaks.

Most drown, and those few spared
die by long starvation.
Everywhere the waters prevail
with no one to be found.

FUTILITIES

A thunderhead builds all day
over the still construction site.

You don't need to know;
I'm not at liberty to say.

■

Across the air shaft, two floors up,
someone blindly searches
the keys of a piano
for "Buffalo Gals,"
rummaging through the wardrobe,
the melody misplaced.

■

In sunlight on the windowsill

Mexican jumping beans
click in their plastic case.

All morning they work
in yesterday's wake,
always a day behind,

combing through data
in an endless effort
to close the loop.

THE WELL

You spend the morning sunk in work
designing a well deep enough
to reach the Jordan Aquifer
two thousand feet below grade,
a source to outlast rivers
and withstand any earthquake.
The whole system's a wet noodle
and doesn't respond to input motion,
but we have to check each frequency.

Amid the toil, you glance up
to find the setting sun
enflaming a glass curtain wall,
still daylight on the highest peak.
Voices rise up from the dark,
a chance encounter at the crosswalk,
friends off to get a drink,
their high, arcing vowels of laughter
receding to a hum.

You pedal home along the lake,
the water's surface cockled

and coriaceous, rimmed with ice.
Tires hiss through wet clay,
muscles taut against the drag
of wind and gravity.

At night you lie in bed
still thinking of the well
and wait beneath a cold sheet
for the brush of fingers
on your skin—then sleep,
boring down through bedrock
to the source of every spring.

Wait with the ache, then start to move
slowly in long and steady strokes,
the soothing yet athletic joy
of rocking hips and humming throat,
with supple shifts in thrust and friction,
a puff in the apparent wind
or momentary lull to trace
a clavicle beneath the skin.
Tongue and fingertips conduct
a mild electric current
that tastes of zinc and stimulates
a tingle, effervescent.
Across the flooded fields, a plover
calls to the approaching rain,
a coiled spring under pressure,
chu-weet! and then *chu-weet!* again,
as patience and impatience
contend, reluctant to succumb,
locked in this compulsion
until released, you come.

ANNABELLE

A white hydrangea trembles
in sodium-vapor light

each crimped petal cut
from taffeta or silk

each inflorescence a flock
or swarm of volatiles

intently feeding
on their milky pedicels

frenzied in sheer detail
like flounces on a camisole

a mop of foam or froth
that crumples at a breath

its full bloom
convulsive as a sneeze

TOMMY JARRELL

This tune, a substitute for talk,
meanders through the morning walk
to work, a whistled rise and fall,
its contour conversational;
a jig, though oftentimes a song
of water tanks and whiskey, drawn
from sources fed by steady rain
and legends of *remote Cockaigne*.
A substitute for Ring Creek
this tune descended from Round Peak,
descending from Mount Airy through
the mic on WPAQ
740 *Merry-Go-Round*
to form a little stream of sound,
an earth- and iron-tinted flow
that rippled from the radio
when we were young. For thirty years
the tune has echoed in my ears.
Though stripped of words, the tones beneath
still whistle softly through my teeth,
the absentminded rise and fall
of voices through a bedroom wall
that blend in sleep until they seem
the murmurs of a little stream.

THE SINKHOLE

Unclenched and half asleep—
bloodstream tinged with melatonin,
the hormonal expression of darkness—
I lie still, listening to a soft
persistent tapping at the baseboard,
the little sounds that demand nothing,
ordain nothing, explain nothing . . .
A mouse worries a curl of wire.
The house settles a hair's breadth,
ground giving way far below
in a bed of porous limestone.
And through the stone, a cavern
meanders for a mile or so
to Uhrig's Cave, a dank saloon
strung with lights, where the chorus sings,
We sail the ocean blue.
A stream of cold air, redolent of soil,
leads on through a mushroom farm
to swimming pools of wet clay,
Penates of brick, and bones
of prehistoric peccaries.
The entrances have long been lost

in basements, behind furnaces,
or sealed with highway rubble.
These birdless regions now permit
no traffic with the surface
but for the secret course of water
and low tones of a gallon jug.

I see my mother's ghost among the dead,
sitting in silence near the blood.
Not once has she glanced this way or spoken:
does she not recognize her son?

Thick drops beat against the glass.
The ceiling plaster ticks, a sound as soft
as a struck match or shutter click.
As my head begins to settle,
days flash behind my lids
without sound—*Lampyridae,*
the cold and shining ones.

DAY IN, DAY OUT

Whatever remembers
won't remember this,
chooses not to,
wants to tell a story
and finds no use
for the day's residue,
stripping down
roman à clef
to epitaph.

Whatever remembers
takes the remnants
out each night
beyond the western gate
and drops them
down a well,
not hidden
from the light,
but altogether gone.

FRANKIE

If you find from the evidence
that on or about the fifteenth day
of October 1899
the plaintiff Frankie Baker killed
one Al, or Allen, or Albert Britt
a conceited piano player
in her home on Targee Street
in the city of Saint Louis

and thereafter said plaintiff
charged with murder in the second degree
was tried and found not guilty,
having shot in self-defense
as Britt came through the door near dawn.
He reached in his pocket, opened his knife,
and started around this side to cut me.
I was staying here. Pillow lays this way.
Just run my hand under the pillow
and shot him. Didn't shoot but once.

And if you further find
Frankie released from the Four Courts

the judge even gave me back my gun
heard as she walked down the steps
and through the gaslit streets
well along toward winter
one Bill Dooley sing and play
the ballad "Frankie Killed Allen"
also known as "Frankie and Johnny"
portraying incidents in her life
now entered into evidence,

and that she fled to Omaha
but heard the song again,
fled it all the way to Portland
and set up in the north end,
first in prostitution
and then a shoeshine parlor.

And if you further find
in May of 1936
the defendants, Republic Pictures,
produced a moving-talking feature
known as *Frankie and Johnnie*
that caused the plaintiff distress,
humiliation, and mental pain
by reason of its false portrayal

of Frankie as a murderess
a fucky hussy, a queen sport
with a razor scar down one cheek,

then and in these events
your verdict may be for the plaintiff.

But if you find and believe
as experts have so testified
that said song was composed and known
prior to 1899,
that *Johnny Died in Song*
Before Targee Street Frankie Shot Him,
with verses sung at the siege of Vicksburg
among the trenches and redoubts,
and that that ballad may in fact
concern one Frankie Silver
who killed her husband with an ax
and hung for it, in another song
My sun goes down, my days are past,
and I must leave this world at last.
The crowd that gathered tore apart
the oak from which she swung
for souvenirs, each taking home
a splinter from the True Cross.

If you find the plaintiff
has no place in song,
that *this story has no moral*
this story has no end,
send her back to Portland
for an honest shine,
let her make an honest dime.
Don't make her a rich woman
because she shot a little boy.

Finally, the court instructs
that there can be no privacy
in what's already public.

PARLOR MUSIC

Advertised in the laundry room,
a Wurlitzer spinet from '46,
abandoned by a tenant
who couldn't make the rent:
The manufacturer calls to mind
a jukebox with its neon arc,
carnivals and carousels,
entertainments cheap and public.
I'm doubtful they made good pianos.
Still, the landlady let it go
for three hundred dollars
and helped me wheel it
down to my unit
where it sits against the wall,
a wardrobe of mahogany wood,
sheet music stored inside the bench
purely aspirational.

My aunt had such an instrument,
an upright polished yet unplayed
in a parlor that no children entered,
couch and armchair covered

with plastic slips, a faint whiff
of lemon Pledge and potpourri.
Through all those years, the lid held
a basket of wax fruit.
Strict and taciturn, my aunt
only sang in church
and kept her daughter away from us,
as we were wild, unsupervised,
and mixed with every sort.
Her shotgun duplex lay within
a ward of silent porches,
lawns overrun
with star-of-Bethlehem,
the local industry reduced
to ring binders and rubber stamps.

After she died, and we all came back
for the funeral, a small affair,
I stripped off the plastic
and stretched out on the couch.
My cousin, then past fifty,
picked up a dusty wax peach
and with a confidential air
turned it over to show me
the imprint of a child's teeth.

THE FALL OF ICARUS

AFTER OVID

Weary of Crete and long exile
and longing to touch his native soil,
Daedalus was islanded
and waterlocked. At length he pondered,
Though Minos blockades land and sea,
the sky above lies open.
We'll go that way. Though he may rule
the earth, he can't control the air.
Back at his bench, the artisan
turned his mind to arts unknown,
tinkering with laws of nature.
He laid out feathers in a row,
from short to long, just as the reeds
of panpipes rise gradually.
He bound these flight feathers with thread
and joined them to the coverts
with wax along the leading edge,
then gave the fabricated wings
the slight curve for lift
he had observed in passing gulls,
learning his craft from real birds.

Icarus, his only boy,
not knowing flight would mean his fall,
stood by and watched with upturned face,
and caught drifting bits of down
or softened the yellow beeswax
between his thumb and finger,
generally underfoot
and hampering his father's work.
Once Daedalus was done,
with the last strut set in place,
he hovered in the pair of wings,
suspended in the air he stirred.

He warned his son, *Icarus!*
fly only in the middle course;
too low, the waves will sink your wings,
too high, and flame will scorch them.
Fly between. Don't navigate
by the Plowman or the Great Bear
or the drawn sword of Orion.
Just follow me. Such were the rules
for flight the father laid down
before he strapped the strange wings
across both their shoulders.
Amid the work and warnings

the old man's cheeks were wet with tears;
his hands shook, and he kissed his boy
for the last time, then flew ahead,
full of fear for his companion.
Just as a falcon leads its young
fledgling from the very lip
of a high nest into thin air,
he urged Icarus to follow
and taught the fatal skills of flight,
flapping his wings and glancing back
to be sure his son did the same.

Some fisherman as he reeled in
his line with trembling rod
or shepherd resting on his staff
or plowman on his stilts
looked up and stood amazed
at those who sailed the skies like gods.
With Delos and Paros in their wake,
and Samos with its vast temple
still a distant smudge to port,
Lebynthos off to starboard,
along with Kalymnos, rich in honey,
the boy began to shed his fear
and find delight in aerobatics.

Abandoning his leader,
drawn by longing for the heights,
he entered a steep climb and stalled.
So close, the fierce rays of the sun
softened the wax that bound his plumes,
releasing a sweet fragrance.
The wax melted: he beat bare arms,
but lacking oars displaced no air,
and with his mouth still forming *da*
of his father's name, he plunged into
the sky-blue mirror of the sea,
the name of which derives from him.

Meanwhile, his worried father—
no longer a father—called and called,
Icarus, where have you gone?
Tell me where to find you!
Calling and calling, *Icarus!*
he saw white feathers on the waves
and cursed his craft, and laid to rest
the body in a beehive tomb
on the island of Icaria,
which still recalls the fallen boy.

PRINCE

The narrow cell contains a bunk,
steel desk mounted on the wall,
toilet, sink, and television;
each cell the same and pervading all
fluorescent light and the smell of bleach.
A window slit admits the sun
to cinder block and concrete.
A kennel, really, without the run.

A new program gives any man
who keeps a clean conduct sheet
a rescue dog to house and train,
along with collar, leash, and crate;
though Prince sleeps on the bottom bunk
(they call him Prince for his Jheri curl)
and patiently awaits the brush,
its soothing motion through his fur
the only licit form of touch
with any living thing beyond
the ritual formality
of bumping fists or shaking hands.

Prince may have some bichon frise
or chow in his heredity,
with features that were bred to please
a Genghis Khan or Medici.
The emperor Ling-ti of Han
appointed chows as chancellors
while soldiers on the Eastern Steppe
slept all winter out of doors.

WILD BIRD RESCUE

A black cat
in search of breakfast

flowed along the path
beneath the hospital window

and by its mute current
woke the mews

from dreams of tearing meat
to irritable molt

a peregrine
aloof and ill at ease

singing a soft *cack-cack*
through wire mesh

restless to row
through a sea of thermals

with the tilting world
reduced to low relief

scars and wrinkles
on a living surface

two thousand feet
two thousand feet below

which raises a problem
the problem of hunger

how vast the empty space
you wish to measure

ABOVE THE
HAWKESBURY

Returning to Mooney Mooney
after three years away,
a thousand nights and days
on the other side of the world,
we find our rental cottage hardly changed,
whatever guests have come and gone;
the wooden Buddha with a broken finger,
the nautical bunks, parts of toys
left in a drawer three years ago,
and through the sliding glass door,
crested pigeons on a telephone line
calling over distance,
Snake Island and the far shore.

As night falls on Illinois
and the home we left unlit,
three black cockatoos
cross the dazed morning:
their flight buoyant and level,
they swim through wedges of sunlight

to settle in frangipani trees
with a weird *wylah wylah*,
calling back the forgotten names.

The sky dims over Ku⁄ring⁄gai,
dysrhythmia of dusk at noon;
the quick hiss of rain,
and within it a deeper rustle,
gives way to splatter on jalousies
as a gutter overflows
and then subsides to pouring sand.

Against the tide's smooth momentum
the island seems to slide upstream.
A bell rings from time to time,
vibrations on the inner ear
from out across the wide water.

Having come through turbulence,
through days and nights in disarray,
we find ourselves
unmoored from habits,
adrift among strange constellations,
Crux and Coalsack Nebula
sunk in a shallow bay.

TWO AUSTRALIAN

LANDSCAPES

I. NEAR LORNE

Heath burnt
down to the beach
with only a bit
of pigface coming back
where William Buckley
the fugitive
slowly starved
on raw mollusks
which the natives
call kooderoo
the kids disperse
and rummage through
rock pools
eroded to honeycomb
for cuttlefish bones
and top shells
spiraling in on themselves
a souvenir

something to take home
at sunset
a gouache of milky surf
as waves blunder against
the concrete pier
no railings
no horizon

II. YOU YANGS

From a hilltop
hump of granite
and black hornblende
the whip
of a distant road
conveys an edge
and the pooling volume
behind that edge
the closed form
of an ocean bed's
transparent stain
with intimations of depth
a dark plain
on which biomorphs
disport themselves
allusive squiggles
or the smear of sudden
movement
spectral with speed
nowhere to stop

no center
in which to stand
only scattered
here and there
in the rain shadow
where no rain falls
she-oaks and gum trees
the ones who wait
the ones who watch

AT FORTY-SIX

In a deck chair
under castellated clouds
Campari and tonic
bitterness
and through damp air
the gleam of a distant lake
the property of stillness
or tang of iron-heavy water
turrets and castellations
September days
with a few acquaintances
talking seldom
and then always
in dry tones
of scuffed gravel
horseradish in vinegar
the snort before a sneeze
a piquant phrase
and wake of laughter
ceruleans
on wooded slopes
along the Cuivre

appetite

without fulfillment

no more outrageous hopes

one mountain pale

beyond another

EDO BOWL

Set on a flared, elevated foot
this sake bowl served
the Floating World:
a little moonlight slid
along the open spout
and out across the lake,
red lacquer worn down
to an undercoat of black.

Overhead a wood duck
sounds the dark, its whine
a thin rise and fall,
a vibrating column of air,
a call that could be carved
from walnut or osage
cut along the Meramec
and fitted with a reed
to draw down the real duck
from wherever it was bound.
Now it glides among the reeds
and through a raft of decoys,
red eye of morning set
in an iridescent whorl.

POEM FOR

THE NEW YEAR

I've tracked myself from day to day
how many steps through a field of snow
how many hours have I slept
what have I eaten
what did I burn
calories or cigarettes
what birds have poured
through Bellefontaine
where mausoleums bear the names
of Busch and Brown
Lemp and Spink
on marble white as winter endive
when I can read my title clear
to mansions in the skies
what have I read
how many words
what facts
statistics biometrics
what data aggregation
what news

of wins and losses
getting and spending
each dawn a color wheel
to gauge the shifting moods
the daylight sunk in trees
an index of attraction

According to the Tao Te Ching
each day brings more
and more of less
less and still less
with no end to nothing
and nothing left undone

Even here in Bellefontaine
along a winding street
silence brings an interval
of yet more distant sound
trucks along the interstate
a plane behind the clouds